Nicolson

by Iain Gray

WRITING *to* REMEMBER

79 Main Street, Newtongrange,
Midlothian EH22 4NA
Tel: 0131 344 0414
E-mail: info@lang-syne.co.uk
www.langsyneshop.co.uk

Design by Dorothy Meikle
Printed by Printwell Ltd
© Lang Syne Publishers Ltd 2023

All rights reserved. No part of this publication may be reproduced, stored or introduced into a retrieval system, or transmitted in any form or by any means (electronic, mechanical, photocopying, recording or otherwise) without the prior written permission of Lang Syne Publishers Ltd.

ISBN 978-1-85217-769-0

Nicolson

MOTTOES:
Generositate (By generosity or By inheritance)
– *Clan Nicolson*
Sgorr-A-Bhreac (Scorrybreac)
– *Clan MacNeacail*

CRESTS:
A lion – *Clan Nicolson*
A hawk's head – *Clan MacNeacail*

TERRITORIES:
The Lowlands – *Clan Nicolson*
Isle of Skye – *Clan MacNeacail*

NAME variations include:
Nicholson   MacNicholas
MacNicol   MacNickle
MacNicoll   MacNeacail

Chapter one:

The origins of the clan system

by Rennie McOwan

The original Scottish clans of the Highlands and the great families of the Lowlands and Borders were gatherings of families, relatives, allies and neighbours for mutual protection against rivals or invaders.

Scotland experienced invasion from the Vikings, the Romans and English armies from the south. The Norman invasion of what is now England also had an influence on land-holding in Scotland. Some of these invaders stayed on and in time became 'Scottish'.

The word clan derives from the Gaelic language term 'clann', meaning children, and it was first used many centuries ago as communities were formed around tribal lands in glens and mountain fastnesses.

The format of clans changed over the centuries, but at its best the chief and his family held the land on behalf of all, like trustees, and the ordinary clansmen and women believed they had a blood relationship with the founder of their clan.

There were two way duties and obligations. An inadequate chief could be deposed and replaced by someone of greater ability.

Clan people had an immense pride in race. Their relationship with the chief was like adult children to a father and they had a real dignity.

The concept of clanship is very old and a more feudal notion of authority gradually crept in.

Pictland, for instance, was divided into seven principalities ruled by feudal leaders who were the strongest and most charismatic leaders of their particular groups.

By the sixth century the 'British' kingdoms of Strathclyde, Lothian and Celtic Dalriada (Argyll) had emerged and Scotland, as one nation, began to take shape in the time of King Kenneth MacAlpin.

Some chiefs claimed descent from ancient kings which may not have been accurate in every case.

By the twelfth and thirteenth centuries the clans and families were more strongly brought under the central control of Scottish monarchs.

Lands were awarded and administered more and more under royal favour, yet the power of the area clan chiefs was still very great.

The long wars to ensure Scotland's

independence against the expansionist ideas of English monarchs extended the influence of some clans and reduced the lands of others.

Those who supported Scotland's greatest king, Robert the Bruce, were awarded the territories of the families who had opposed his claim to the Scottish throne.

In the Scottish Borders country – the notorious Debatable Lands – the great families built up a ferocious reputation for providing warlike men accustomed to raiding into England and occasionally fighting one another.

Chiefs had the power to dispense justice and to confiscate lands and clan warfare produced a society where martial virtues – courage, hardiness, tenacity – were greatly admired.

Gradually the relationship between the clans and the Crown became strained as Scottish monarchs became more orientated to life in the Lowlands and, on occasion, towards England.

The Highland clans spoke a different language, Gaelic, whereas the language of Lowland Scotland and the court was Scots and in more modern times, English.

Highlanders dressed differently, had different

customs, and their wild mountain land sometimes seemed almost foreign to people living in the Lowlands.

It must be emphasised that Gaelic culture was very rich and story-telling, poetry, piping, the clarsach (harp) and other music all flourished and were greatly respected.

Highland culture was different from other parts of Scotland but it was not inferior or less sophisticated.

Central Government, whether in London or Edinburgh, sometimes saw the Gaelic clans as a challenge to their authority and some sent expeditions into the Highlands and west to crush the power of the Lords of the Isles.

Nevertheless, when the eighteenth century Jacobite Risings came along the cause of the Stuarts was mainly supported by Highland clans.

The word Jacobite comes from the Latin for James – Jacobus. The Jacobites wanted to restore the exiled Stuarts to the throne of Britain.

The monarchies of Scotland and England became one in 1603 when King James VI of Scotland (1st of England) gained the English throne after Queen Elizabeth died.

The Union of Parliaments of Scotland and England, the Treaty of Union, took place in 1707.

Some Highland clans, of course, and Lowland families opposed the Jacobites and supported the incoming Hanoverians.

After the Jacobite cause finally went down at Culloden in 1746 a kind of ethnic cleansing took place. The power of the chiefs was curtailed. Tartan and the pipes were banned in law.

Many emigrated, some because they wanted to, some because they were evicted by force. In addition, many Highlanders left for the cities of the south to seek work.

Many of the clan lands became home to sheep and deer shooting estates.

But the warlike traditions of the clans and the great Lowland and Border families lived on, with their descendants fighting bravely for freedom in two world wars.

Remember the men from whence you came, says the Gaelic proverb, and to that could be added the role of many heroic women.

The spirit of the clan, of having roots, whether Highland or Lowland, means much to thousands of people.

Meanwhile, many families proudly boast the heraldic device known as a Coat of Arms,.

The central motif of the Coat of Arms would originally have been what was sometimes borne on the shield of a warrior to distinguish himself from others on the battlefield.

Clan warfare produced a society where courage and tenacity were greatly admired

Chapter two:

Raids and Risings

A surname with religious roots, 'Nicolson' and its popular spelling variant 'Nicholson', both denoting 'son of Nicolas/Nicholas', stem from reverence for a fourth century Christian bishop of the name which, in turn, derives from the Greek forename *Nikolaos*, meaning 'conqueror of the people' or 'victory people.'

In Scotland, it is unusual in that the name relates to two separate clans.

These are the Lowland Clan Nicolson and the Highland Clan MacNicol, more properly known in Gaelic as Clan MacNeacail – with 'Mac' denoting 'son of' and 'Neacail' an Anglicisation of 'Nicolas/Nicholas'.

Before travelling back through the dim mists of time to unravel their separate origins, it's useful to back-track a few years from the present to the mid-1980s.

This was when the Lord Lyon King of Arms of Scotland – the ultimate arbiter on matters genealogical and heraldic – formally recognised

David Nicolson, 4th Baron Carnock, as Chief of Clan Nicolson and Iain MacNeacail of MaNeacail and Scorrybreac as Chief of Clan MacNeacail.

The MacNeacails, meanwhile, had adopted the Anglicised form of their name in the late seventeenth century, but the Lord Lyon King of Arms stipulated that to make clear their separation from Clan Nicolson, they should adopt the 'MacNeacail' form in heraldic matters.

In keeping with their separate heritage and traditions, their chiefly Coat of Arms differ.

The heraldic crest of Clan Nicolson features a lion and the Latin motto *Generositate*, meaning 'by generosity' or 'by inheritance', while the MacNeacail crest is a hawk's head and the Gaelic motto *Sgorr-A-Bhreac*, referencing their ancestral lands of Scorrybreac, in Trotternish on the Isle of Skye.

Intriguingly, however, the central motif of their Coat of Arms are similar, in that they both feature a gold shield with birds of prey – hawks for the MacNeacails and falcons for the Nicolsons.

But authorities nevertheless stress there is no evidence to support a genealogical link between their respective chiefly lines.

Even more intriguingly is that flowing

through the veins of some descendants of both clans today is a rich and heady brew of the blood of Norsemen.

In the case of the MacNeacails, this bloodline is also enriched by that of those Gaels who first arrived and settled on the western seaboard of Scotland from Ireland and established the kingdom of *Dál Riata*, or Dalriada, that included parts of both countries.

Norsemen such as the Vikings and Scandinavian Danes, meanwhile, first began their bloody raids into Scotland in the eighth century, but many eventually abandoned their feared long ships in favour of settlement – intermixing with the native race such as those who would come to bear the MacNeacail name.

Despite their Norse heritage the MacNeacails, in common with other clans of the western seaboard with Norse ancestry, fought for Scotland's cause during the Scottish-Norwegian War of 1262 to 1266 – a conflict over the ownership of the Hebrides.

In 1098, King Edgar of Scotland had ceded control of the Hebrides to Norway's King Magnus III, with the Norwegians also tightening their control over the Orkneys and the Isle of Man.

During the reign of Scotland's King Alexander III, attempts were made to buy the Hebrides from the Norwegians but these proved fruitless.

However, in 1262, under Alexander, Norway's King Haakon IV was told if he still refused to sell the lands, they would be taken by force.

Warned that Alexander was prepared to wrest the islands from Norwegian control, Haakon embarked with a mighty fleet from Bergen in July of 1263.

His fierce band of sea raiders plundered and ravaged Kintyre, Bute and Islay, before appearing off the west coast mainland township of Largs.

A storm blew many of the vessels onto the shore beneath the overhanging Cunningham hills on the night of September 30, and it was on top of these hills that the Scots king hastily assembled a force of militia.

They emerged from their high eminence the following morning and engaged in a skirmish with a band of Norsemen attempting to salvage precious cargo from their stricken vessels – but the Scots drove them back to their ships and returned that evening to gleefully loot the cargo.

Stung by the insult, King Haakon ordered a further attempt to retrieve the cargo the following day,

October 1, resulting in what has become known as the battle of Largs but which in reality consisted of a series of disorganised skirmishes.

The Norsemen were driven back to their vessels, however, and Haakon died a few weeks later in Kirkwall, Orkney.

The threat to Scotland's western seaboard in general and invasion of the mainland in particular had been averted, while the battle is commemorated annually at Largs with the ceremonial burning of a Viking longboat.

It was as reward for their role in the battle, having brought their war galleys into decisive play, that the MacNeacails were gifted with Scorrybreac Castle, also known as Scorrybreac House, on Skye.

Located on the isle's northernmost peninsula of Trotternish, Scorrybreac's 130 acres of ground were bought by the International Clan MacNeacail Federation in 1987 and feature a magnificent nature trail around Ben Chracaig known as the Scorrybreac Trails.

Skye, meanwhile, once part of the Gaelic-Norse Kingdom of the Isles, was where Clan MacNeacail flourished for centuries, while tradition holds their previous territory had been Lewis.

They appear in the historical record in the early fourteenth century in the person of John 'mak Naykl' who, in the early years of the First War of Scottish Independence from 1296 to 1328 initially lent his support to England's King Edward I.

But two years after Robert the Bruce's victory at the battle of Bannockburn in 1314, it is possible that this is the same person recorded as being present with Nigel Bruce, the great warrior king's brother, at the siege of Carrickfergus Castle, as part of the campaign to take the war against Edward to Ireland.

Still on the wider stage of turbulent Scottish affairs in particular and that of the British Isles in general, Clan MacNeacail also played a role in the bitter and bloody seventeenth century wars between Crown and Covenant by supporting the Royalist cause and fighting at the side of the ill-fated James Graham, 1st Marquis of Montrose.

In the following century, after the 'Glorious Revolution' of 1688 that saw the flight into exile of King James II (King James VII of Scotland) and the accession to the throne of William of Orange and his wife Mary, the church minister Donald Nicolson of Scorrybreac, also chief of the clan, refused to swear allegiance to the new king.

As a Jacobite, as supporters of the Royal House of Stuart were known, he was driven from his parish by the authorities – but left a notable legacy.

Reputed to have fathered no fewer than 23 children, he is thought to be a common ancestor of a substantial number of families on Skye to this day.

During the 1745 Jacobite Rising, the MacNeacails/Nicolsons did not formally rally as a clan to Charles Edward Stuart, better known to posterity as Bonnie Prince Charlie, but some enlisted in the ranks of those who fought at the disastrous battle of Culloden in April of 1746.

Following the prince's defeat and subsequent 'flight through the heather', he is known to have received aid and shelter from the clan on Skye.

The clan chief, John Nicolson, hid him for a while in a cow byre, while his descendants to this day preserve a lock of his hair and a cup from which he drank.

Margaret Nicolson, a grand-daughter of the Rev Donald Nicolson, also aided the prince, while Donald Nicolson of Raasay was tortured by government troops for refusing to reveal his whereabouts.

Chapter three:

Honours and distinction

In common with their MacNeacail counterparts in the Highlands and Islands, the Lowland Clan Nicolson also have a Norse bloodline – but through a different means of infusion.

It is highly probable they were among those Anglo-Normans who began to settle in Scotland during the reign from 1124 to 1153 of King David I who, during English exile for a time, had become enamoured with Norman customs, military and organisational skills and enterprise and, accordingly, held out the lure of settling in Scotland by offering them lands.

It is not known with certainty where those who would come to bear the Nicolson name originally settled after their migration from south of the border, but it is reasonable to assume it was in Aberdeenshire.

It is in Aberdeen that they held the important civic role of burgesses, while the chiefly line of the clan stems from one of their descendants, James Nicolson, an Edinburgh lawyer who died in about 1580.

He, in turn, had two sons – James and John – with the former a prominent churchman who was appointed Bishop of Dunkeld a year before his death in 1607, having earlier served as Moderator of the Church of Scotland.

His older brother John Nicolson, who held the lands of Lasswade, Midlothian, died in 1605 – while his son Sir Thomas Nicolson, styled Nicolson of that Ilk and Lasswade, was created a Baronet of Nova Scotia in 1637.

His date of birth is not known, but records show he worked from 1612 as an advocate and, through the influence of John Murray, 1st Earl of Annandale, served in the office of postmaster at Cockburnspath, in the Borders.

He purchased Carnock House, near Stirling, in 1634 and it was three years later he was created Baronet Nicolson, of Carnock, County of Stirling.

The baronetcy was granted through the Order of Baronets of Nova Scotia, which has a rather unusual genesis.

Knighted in 1609 by King James I (James VI of Scotland), fellow Scot Sir William Alexander of Menstrie had approached his monarch with a potentially lucrative proposal – to offer, for cash, a new order of baronets to encourage the development of a 'New Scotland' (Nova Scotia) in foreign climes.

Amenable to this, James signed a grant in favour of Sir William that covered all the lands "Between our Colonies of New England and New Foundland, to be known as New Scotland".

This was a vast area – now one of Canada's three maritime provinces – and the king followed the grant up with an announcement of his intention to create a new order of baronets open to 'knights and gentlemen.'

The king died in 1625, but his successor King Charles I almost immediately put his father's plan into action – with the first 22 Baronets created by the end of the year.

In parallel to this, Sir William Alexander offered tracts of land to (translated from the original) 'all such principal knights and squires as will be pleased to be undertakers of the said plantations and who will promise to set forth six men, artificers or labourers, sufficiently armed, apparelled and victualled for two years.'

Patents for their land and the all-important elevation to the peerage of Great Britain and Ireland as Barons of Nova Scotia were granted – while a special arrangement was improvised for those not able to travel to receive them in the royal court in London.

This involved a special ceremony on the esplanade of Edinburgh Castle, for which to serve heraldic protocol only on the day was declared to be 'Nova Scotia'.

In this early example of 'cash for honours', the enterprising Sir William Alexander extracted a fee of 1,000 merks – equivalent to approximately £6,000 in today's terms – for his 'past work in discovery of the said country.'

But the colonisation scheme quickly foundered, with many settlers killed through exposure to the harsh climate, while its final death knell was sounded in 1632 when the king ceded the lands to King Louis XIII of France and ordered the removal of the surviving settlers and the destruction of Charles Fort, at Port Royal.

Nevertheless, although the colonisation scheme had proven an abysmal failure rather bizarrely grants of land were still being made until 1639, while the baronetcies were still being granted up until 1707.

In total, 329 baronetcies were conferred since

the inception of the Order of Baronets of Nova Scotia, including that granted to Sir Thomas Nicolson of Carnock in 1637.

He died in 1646, while his descendants went on to achieve high honours and distinction of their own, as the inherited baronetcy title continued through the family line.

These include Thomas Nicolson, 4th Baronet, born in 1669 and who died in 1688 and who also became, through inheritance, 4th Lord Napier of Merchistoun.

In a much later century, there is the diplomat and politician Sir Arthur Nicolson, 11th Baronet and who was also elevated to the peerage as 1st Baron Carnock – the titles 'Baronet' and 'Baron', it should be noted, are quite distinct.

Born in 1849, the son of Admiral Sir Frederick Nicolson, 10th Baronet and his wife Mary, née Loch, he joined the Foreign Office in 1870, serving there for four years and during which time he wrote *History of the German Constitution*.

Later Secretary of the British Embassy at Berlin, followed by Secretary at the Embassy of Peking from 1876 to 1878, subsequent high profile foreign postings included Chargé d'affairs in Teheran from 1885 to 1888 and, from 1895 to 1904, British Minister at Tangiers.

Having succeeded his father as Baronet of Carnock in 1899 and also serving as British Ambassador to Russia and, from 1910 to 1916 as Permanent Under-Secretary for Foreign Affairs, he was raised to the peerage in 1916 as Baron Carnock, of Carnock in the County of Stirling.

He died in 1928, while one of his sons was Erskine "Eric" Nicolson, who succeeded his older brother Frederick as 3rd Baron following his death in 1952.

Born in 1884 and educated at the Royal Naval College, Dartmouth, he served as a staff officer during the First World War on a light cruiser squadron, and was the recipient of many honours including Chevalier of the Legion d'honneur and the Distinguished Service Order.

He died in 1982, while he was the older brother of the colourful diplomat, politician, author and diarist Sir Harold Nicolson and his wife the equally colourful fellow writer Vita Sackville-West.

Born in 1886, and in common with his father, he embarked on a career with the Foreign Office followed by the Diplomatic Service, holding posts including Third Secretary at Constantinople from 1912 until the outbreak of war in 1914.

Serving in the Foreign Office during the conflict as Second Secretary and after the war as First Secretary, he served during the Second World War as official Censor at the Ministry of Information.

As a politician, for a short period before the Second World War he supported Sir Oswald Mosley and his New Party, but ended the association when Mosley founded the British Union of Fascists and, in 1935, he entered the House of Commons as MP (Member of Parliament) for Leicester West for the National Labour Party.

In addition to his career as a diplomat, politician and writer of noted works including studies of literary figures such as Tennyson, Swinburne, Byron and the French poet Verlaine, he is also remembered for his often tempestuous marriage to Victoria Mary Sackville-West, Lady Nicolson, better known as Vita Sackville-West.

The couple married in 1913 and, both bisexual, maintained what was very much an open marriage, with husband and wife having affairs with a number of lovers.

But despite this, the couple remained happy together.

Vita, born in 1892, was a highly successful poet, journalist, diarist and the recipient on two occasions of the prestigious Hawthornden Prize for Imaginative Literature – in 1927 for her epic *The Land* and, in 1933, for her *Collected Poems*.

An inspiration for her friend and lover Virginia Woolf's novel *Orlando: A Biography*, she was also an accomplished garden designer and, when she and her husband acquired Sissinghurst Castle, near Cranbrook, Kent, in the 1930s, the couple created the magnificent gardens there that are now maintained by the National Trust.

She died in 1962, while her husband died six years later.

Chapter four:
On the world stage

From literature and sport to the stage and science, bearers of the Nicolson name and its popular spelling variant 'Nicholson' have gained recognition and distinction.

A co-founder of the Weidenfeld and Nicolson publishing house, **Nigel Nicolson** was the writer and politician born in Kent in 1917.

The second son of Sir Harold Nicolson and Vita Sackville-West, it was along with George Weidenfeld that in 1949 he founded Weidenfeld and Nicolson, serving as a director until 1992.

Having served during the Second World War with the Grenadier Guards, he went on to write their official history.

His most celebrated book, *Portrait of a Marriage*, a candid account of his bisexual parents' extra-marital affairs, caused a sensation when first published in 1979.

As a Conservative Party politician, serving as MP for Bournemouth East and Christchurch from 1952 to 1959, he was on occasion out of step with mainstream party opinion – voting with the Labour Party, for example, to abolish capital punishment.

A columnist for the *Spectator* magazine and the *Sunday Telegraph*, he died seven years after the publication in 1997 of his autobiography *Long Life*.

Married to Philippa, the daughter of Sir Gervais Tennyson d'Eyncourt, he was the father of the historian Julia Nicolson, the journalist Rebecca Nicolson and the writer Adam Nicolson.

His older brother Benedict Nicolson, better known as **Ben Nicolson**, was the art historian and author born in 1914.

Appointed Deputy Surveyor of the King's Pictures in 1939, he held the post for only a short time before serving with the Intelligence Corps during the Second World War.

Resuming the post with the royal household after the war – serving under Anthony Blunt, who was later unmasked as a Soviet spy – he subsequently edited the *Burlington* magazine in addition to collecting photographs of early seventeenth century paintings in the style of Caravaggio.

He died in 1978, while he was the uncle of the writer **Adam Nicolson, 5th Baron Carnock**.

Born in 1957 and having inherited the title on

the death of his cousin **David Nicolson, 4th Baron Carnock**, in 2008, but choosing not to use it, he is an award-winning author on subjects ranging from history and literature to landscapes and the sea.

The recipient of awards including the 2004 Royal Society of Literature Heinemann Award for *Power and Glory*, along with his son Tom Nicolson and in collaboration with bodies including the Royal Society for the Protection of Birds (RSPB), he was involved in a project between 2012 and 2017 to rid the Shiant Isles, in the Outer Hebrides, of invasive predators such as rats.

In partnership with the National Trust, between 2005 and 2009 he led a project to transform land surrounding the house and garden at Sissinghurst – first developed by his grandparents – into a mixed farm producing vegetables, cereals, fruit and meat for use in the adjoining National Trust restaurant.

Helping him in this endeavour was his wife Sarah Raven, the gardener, cook, writer and television presenter born in Cambridge in 1963.

On American shores, **Marjorie Nicolson** was the distinguished literary scholar born in 1894 in Yonkers, New York.

The recipient in 1920 of a doctorate in

literature from Yale University and the first woman to receive its prestigious John Addison Porter Prize for her dissertation, she worked for a time as drama critic for the *Detroit Free Press*, where her father Charles Nicolson was editor-in-chief.

Dean and professor from 1929 to 1941 at Smith College, Massachusetts and later the first female graduate school professor at Columbia University and chairman of its graduate department of English and Comparative Literature, her many works include *The Art of Description*, first published in 1937.

A Fellow of the American Academy of Arts and Sciences and the recipient in 1971 of the Science Fiction Research Association's Pilgrim Award for her pioneering work on the relationship between literature and science, she died in 1981.

Bearers of the Nicolson name, in the form of the variant 'Nicholson', have also excelled in the highly competitive world of sport.

In the world of darts, **Paul Nicholson** is the player who defeated fellow Englishman Mervyn King in the final of the 2010 Players Championship.

Born in 1979 in Newcastle upon Tyne, known for coming on stage wearing sunglasses and nicknamed "The Asset", he is also a radio and television sporting pundit.

From darts to football, **Barry Nicholson**, born in Dumfries in 1978, is the Scottish former midfielder who, in addition to playing for his national team, played for clubs including Rangers, Aberdeen, Kilmarnock and Fleetwood Town and acted as caretaker manager for the latter club's first team squad.

In English football, **Bill Nicholson**, born in Scarborough in 1919, was the player, scout, coach and manager best known for his association over a 36-year period as a player and manager with Tottenham Hotspur. An inductee of the English Football Hall of Fame, he died in 2004, while it was under his management that Tottenham Hotspur lifted titles including the FA Cup on three occasions and the 1971-72 Cup Winners' Cup.

From sport to the stage, **Gerda Nicolson** was the Australian theatre and television actress best known for her role from 1983 until 1989 of Governor Ann Reynolds in the popular soap *Prisoner*, having had the role of a corrupt officer at another prison in previous episodes.

Born in 1937 in Hobart, Tasmania and having appeared in other television shows including the police drama *Bluey*, she died in 1992 after collapsing in her dressing room shortly before she was due to go on stage in a theatre production.

From the stage to music, **Anne-Marie Nicholson** is the singer-songwriter nominated for four awards to date, including Best British Female Solo Artist at the 2019 Brit Awards.

Born in 1991 in East Tilbury, Essex, her best-selling albums include the 2018 *Speak Your Mind*.

Taking to the heavens, **Seth Barnes Nicholson** was the American astronomer credited with having discovered a number of moons of Jupiter, including Lysithea and Carme, both in 1938 and, in 1951, Ananke.

Born in 1891 in Springfield, Illinois, based throughout his career at Mount Wilson Observatory, California and, along with fellow astronomer George Ellery Hale responsible for the Hale-Nicholson Law concerning the magnetic polarity of sunspots, he died in 1963.

In the equally complex realms of mathematics, **Phyllis Nicolson** was the married name of the leading British mathematician born Phyllis Lockett in Macclesfield in 1917.

Responsible along with her colleague at

Leeds University, John Crank, for the algorithm known as the Crank-Nicolson method concerning heat equations, she died in 1968.

From mathematics to botany, **Dan Nicolson** was the American botanist born in 1933 in Kansas City, Missouri.

Known for his contribution to the process of naming and classifying botanical specimens and research botanist at the Smithsonian Institution's National Museum of Natural History from 1964 until 2007, he died in 2016.

One particularly colourful bearer of the Nicolson name was **Adela Nicolson**, the married name of the English poet born Adela Cory in Stoke Bishop, Gloucestershire in 1865.

Leaving for India when aged 16 to join her father Colonel Arthur Cory and her mother and two sisters, she soon became immersed in Indian culture.

Employed by the British Army at Lahore, her father was editor of the Lahore section of the *Civil and Military Gazette*, and is credited with having given a young Rudyard Kipling his first job in journalism.

Adela, meanwhile, married Colonel Malcolm Hassels Nicolson – who was almost twice her age – in 1889.

Commandant of the 3rd Battalion, the Baluch Regiment, he already had a reputation for eccentricity and acts of derring-do – on one memorable occasion crossing a river by hopping from one crocodile's back to another.

Joining her husband in his escapades, the equally bold Adela was on the Zhob Valley expedition of 1890, following him through the passes of India's border with Afghanistan dressed as a Pathan Boy.

Fascinated by the Indian poets and the Sufi poets of Persia, in 1901 and under the pseudonym 'Laurence Hope' she launched *Garden of Kama*, published a year later in the United States as *India's Love Lyrics* – but claiming they were her translations of other poets.

It soon transpired, however, that the poems were all her own work, and she became one of the most popular romantic poets of the Edwardian era.

Following the death of her husband, she took her own life in 1904, aged 39, while in 1922 her son Malcolm Nicolson posthumously published her *Selected Poems*.